CONTENTS

This book was produced at the instigation of Charan Burapharat, the Governor of the Expressway and Rapid Transit Authority of Thailand, and its production was made possible by contributions from the following organizations: Expressway and Rapid Transit Authority of Thailand, Hitachi Zosen Corporation, Chor Karnchang Tokyu Construction, Maeda Construction Co., Siam Machinery and Equipment Co., Thyssen Draht AG, Mahajak Industry Co., Kin Sun Onward Co., STS Engineering Consultants Co., Freeman Fox Ltd., 3 F Engineering Consultants Co., Nissho Iwai Corporation, CIS (Paris) SA.

THE BRIDGE IN BRIEF

A RECORD ACHIEVEMENT

The Bangkok Cable-stayed Bridge is a record-breaking engineering achievement. It is the world's largest bridge of its type and is likely to remain so for some time to come. But it is also a remarkable achievement in many other respects.

Considering its size and location it was constructed in an extremely short period. Construction began in October 1984 and was finished three years later in time for the official opening in November 1987. The opening date was part of the celebrations to mark the 60th Birthday of His Majesty King Bhumibol Adulyadej. The completion of the bridge was the last step in the building of the first phase of Bangkok's elevated Expressway system.

The bridge is the lowest bridging point on the Chao Phraya River and the most southerly crossing between the eastern and western sides of Greater Bangkok. The river crossing is a single plane symmetric cable-stayed bridge with a length of 782 meters composed of a 450 meter main span and two 166 meter side spans. Including the concrete approaches that lead to the steel bridge the overall length is three kilometers.

The need for a river crossing for the Expressway in the area of Wat Sai required a structure that would give clearance for ocean-going ships to reach wharves further up the river. The design of the bridge gives a clearance of 41 meters above highest water level. The supports for the bridge are situated on the banks and give a clear span over the river, thereby avoiding the possibility of a ship colliding with one of the supports.

In terms of technology transfer the bridge has accomplished what many considered impossible. All the structural steelwork was made in Thailand and, with the exception of three Japanese crane drivers, the bridge was built solely by Thai construction workers.

It also represents a fine example of international cooperation on behalf of the designers, construction supervisors, contractors and subcontractors. These comprised German, British, American, Japanese, French and Thai companies and personnel.

The bridge was designed by Dr. Ing. Hellmut Homberg of West Germany, a pioneer of cable-stayed bridge development. The construction supervisors were a Consultants' Joint Venture led by Peter Fraenkel International of London who also designed the approach bridges and connecting roads. Parsons Brinckerhoff International of New York provided additional supervision staff as did the local partner of the Joint Venture, National Engineering Consultants Co., Ltd. (NECCO) of Bangkok. After Dr. Homberg withdrew from the project, Freeman Fox Ltd. of London were taken on by the Joint Venture and given responsibility for all aspects of the main span erection and for changes affecting the permanent design.

The contractor for the main bridge was a joint venture whose lead partner was Hitachi Zosen Corporation of Japan. For fabrication of the steelwork and its erection their subcontractor was Siam Machinery and Equipment, a member of the Italian-Thai Group, who established a completely new fabrication factory for the project. The substructure contractor was an established joint venture of a local firm, Chor Karnchang, with Tokyu Construction of Japan. Maeda Construction of Japan were the contractor for both approach bridges as well as for the interchange at the western end of the Expressway.

COMPARISON WITH OTHER BRIDGES

For someone unfamiliar with civil engineering terms "single plane cable-stayed bridge" may cause some difficulties. Many people think the new Bangkok bridge is a suspension bridge. The mistake is understandable because in both cable-stayed and suspension bridges the structure that carries the road, known as the "bridge deck", is supported by cables.

The most simple and most common type of bridge is the beam bridge. It is similar to a plank laid across a stream. The modern arch bridge is not unlike the brick and stone bridges that predated the steel era. The bridge deck rests on, or hangs from, an arch that distributes the weight, or "load", outwards. Arched bridges are well suited to bridging a ravine or chasm with steep solid walls. The walls of the chasm act as "abutments" and absorb the outwardly distributed weight.

A suspension bridge consists of two cables strung over two towers and the bridge deck hangs from these cables. With a suspension bridge the load pulls the cable "anchorages" at either end of the bridge inwards. All of the world's longest clear span bridges are of the suspension type.

On a cable-stayed bridge the deck is supported by cables connected directly to pylons or towers. The load of a cable-stayed bridge presses down on the pylons and piers that support them. There is no overall inward or outward pull because the cables pull against the bridge deck itself and balance out.

A suspension bridge and an arch bridge were considered for the crossing but a cable-stayed design was found to be the most economic mainly because of the local soil conditions. Bangkok is built on layers of clay and sand and the whole city is slowly sinking, the top layer sinking more rapidly than the lower ones.

To build a suspension bridge would have required making concrete anchorages which would have been difficult to fix firmly in the soil because they would begin to sink and move laterally. An arch bridge of the size would have required building large abutments and these would have created problems similar to the anchorages needed for a suspension bridge.

With the cable-stayed design the load on the pylons and piers is supported by piles driven deep into clay and sand layers. As the lower layers sink so does the bridge. The problem of lateral anchorage or abutment movement does not occur with a cable-stayed configuration.

Cabled stayed bridges are of two types. The most common is the double plane type. In this design there are two towers or pylons at each end of the bridge. From the towers twin cables are connected to the sides of the bridge deck. In a single plane design there is only one pylon at each end of the bridge and the cables extending from this are connected to the center of the bridge deck.

In terms of estimated cost, the difference between a single plane and a double plane design for the new bridge was negligible. The single plane design was chosen because it was considered neat and more elegant. It was also thought that the single plane configuration would be easier to erect and subsequent events confirmed this.

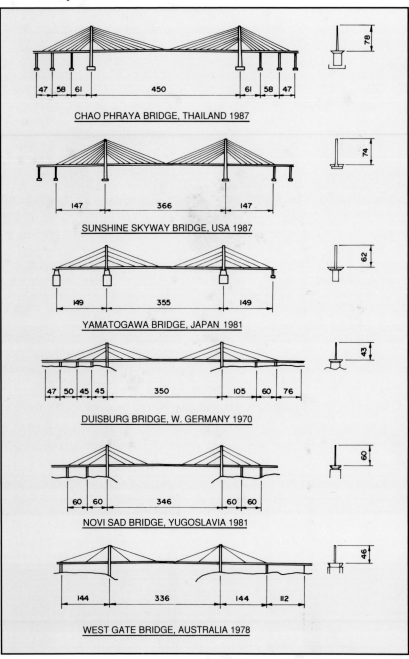

The world's longest single plane cable-stayed bridges

THE EXPRESSWAY

THE GROWTH OF BANGKOK TRAFFIC

Two hundred years ago, when Bangkok was founded, the primary form of transport in Thailand was by river and canal. At that time the low lying area by the Chao Phraya River was an idea site for a capital city. Modern Bangkok has grown around the original system of canals. Except for those used for drainage most of the canals have been replaced by major arterial roads but the lanes leading to these roads still exist as narrow dead-ended access roads. The result is a lack of a secondary street system to service the major roads. Consequently traffic management systems used in other cities, such as one way street operations, have only been successful to a limited extent.

Despite difficult soil conditions and flood problems, Bangkok is still well situated. Being roughly at the center of the country, the major highways and the rail system converge naturally on the city. It is also Thailand's largest port, accommodating inward and outward cargoes of about five million tonnes a year. Other ports are being developed and planned but Bangkok will undoubtedly remain Thailand's major port for the foreseeable future.

Being the administrative, commercial and industrial center of Thailand, Bangkok has undergone a tremendous population increase in this century. In 1900 the population was 460,000, by 1954 it had reached two million, and in the following twenty years the population doubled to four million. The present population of Bangkok is generally estimated at six million.

Thailand's growing prosperity in the last 30 years has led to the ownership of an increasingly large number of passenger cars. There were 67,000 passenger cars registered in Bangkok in 1965. In 1975 the number was estimated at 220,000 and by 1985 the number had reached 560,000. In addition to passenger cars there were 480,000 motorcycles, and a grand total of 1,180,000 private passenger vehicles of all types registered in Bangkok in 1985. Many vehicles registered in Bangkok are not in fact used by Bangkok residents but nor does the registration figure include state owned public transport or represent the heavy use of Bangkok's roads by commercial trucks.

In 1970 it was evident that Bangkok traffic congestion was reaching saturation levels and a major highway planning and construction programme became a matter of the highest priority for the government of Thailand.

ESTABLISHMENT OF ETA

A long-term solution for the traffic problem was required and for this reason the Bangkok Transportation Study was commissioned in 1970/71 by the National Economic and Social Development Board (NESDB). The chosen consultants, a German group, were called upon to prepare a Transport Master Plan for Greater Bangkok to meet contemporary needs and future requirements to the year 1990. This study and plan has been generally referred to as the O.M.T.P Study.

It was realized that a new governmental organization would facilitate the implementation of the Transport Master Plan and in 1972 the Expressway and Rapid Transit Authority of Thailand (ETA) was established as a state enterprise under the Ministry of the Interior. ETA was given responsibility for the investigation, design, construction and toll operation of expressways and mass transit systems throughout the country.

The O.M.T.P. study was completed in 1975 and resulted in a recommendation for the provision of a mass rapid transit system and for the construction of a system of expressways. For the expressways the study identified necessary links between three inter-city highways from various parts of the country (Din Daeng - Don Muang, Bang Na - Trat and Thon Buri - Pak Tho) as forming the backbone of a future Expressway system and that an urban Expressway should link these highways.

In the same year Freeman Fox and Partners in association with Thai Engineering Consultants Co., Ltd. were commissioned by ETA to undertake a preliminary design and feasibility study of the urban Expressway. The first phase Expressway was by then

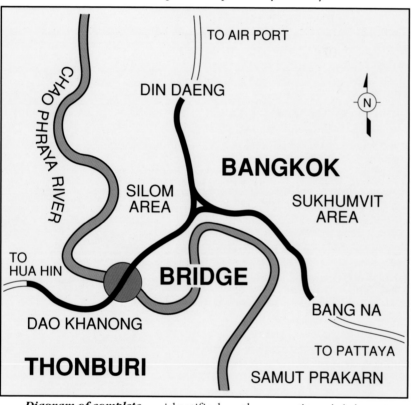

Diagram of complete expressway, First Phase

identified as three sections joining at the Port area of Klong Toey. These were Din Daeng - Port, Port - Bang Na and Port - Dao Khanong. Freeman Fox and Thai Engineering Consultants also undertook the detailed design of the first two sections.

OUTLINE OF THE FIRST PHASE

The first section to be completed was Din Daeng - Port. This links the Port and major thoroughfares in the city with the ten-lane Viphavadi Rangsit Superhighway leading to Don Muang international airport and highways 1 and 2 extending to the North and Northeast of Thailand. This 8.9 kilometer section was opened in January 1982. Following the opening of this section, the First Stage of the Expressway was given the official title of 'Chalerm Maha Nakorn Expressway' by His Majesty the King.

The second section extended the Expressway from the Port to Bang Na. At Bang Na the Expressway joins two highways. One leads to the heavily industrialized area of Samut Prakarn. The other, ultimately leads to Trat (which is southeast of Bangkok near the Kampuchean boarder) and also links with highways to the deep water port at Sattahip and Eastern Seaboard Development Project and Petrochemical Complex in the Rayong area. Opened to traffic in January 1983 this section is 7.9 kilometers long.

The cable-stayed bridge and associated links complete the Port - Dao Khanong section, which is the third and longest section (10.3 kilometers) of the First Stage Expressway System. It links the Expressway to the western (Thon Buri) side of the river and also with Highway 35 which stretches to Pak Tho where it joins Highway 4 leading to the South of Thailand and Malaysia.

The Expressway is 28 meters wide consisting of six lanes (three in each direction) plus emergency lanes for broken-down vehicles. Emergency telephones are situated at kilometer intervals along the entire 27.1 kms. length. Closed-circuit television monitors the system to facilitate traffic control. The system is elevated through most of its length.

ETA OPERATIONS

The ETA obtains revenue by charging tolls for private and commercial vehicles using the Expressway. However, the ETA is set up to provide a public service rather than to make a profit. The revenue from tolls is used to cover the cost of maintenance and amortize the loans used for construction. In 1985 fiscal year there were 45 million journeys made on the Expressway which generated an income of over 506 million baht.

COMPLETING THE FIRST PHASE

The detailed design for the final section of the First Phase was divided into two parts. Part 1 was for the river crossing, the approaches to the crossing and the first interchange (Suksawat interchange) on the Thon Buri side. Part 2 was for sections of the Expressway leading from the Port to the approaches and for sections connecting the Suksawat interchange with the Thon Buri - Pak Tho Highway. At that time it was not known whether the crossing would be

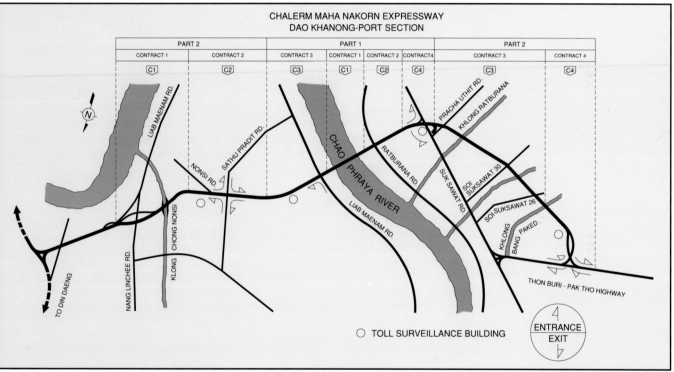

First Phase Expressway, Dao Khanong - Port section

A mass transit system, in the form of an elevated railway in central Bangkok, will be the ETA's next major project. The feasibility study and detailed engineering design were started at the same time as that of the first stage Expressway. The Part 1 Stage 1 will consist of a line running from the Sathorn intersection to Lard Prao and a second line running from Phra Khanong through Sathorn, Hua Lumpong and Bang Sue to the Northern bus terminus on Phaholyothin Road.

The Second Phase of the Expressway is currently in the feasibility and design stage.

a bridge or a tunnel.

Asia Engineering Consultants Corp., Ltd. were commissioned to undertake the detailed design and draw up the tender documents for Part 2. They also acted as the Supervision Engineer during construction. The Obhayashi Corporation was the contractor for all four of the Part 2 contracts.

PLANNING THE BRIDGE

DESIGN CONSIDERATIONS

The Harbour Department and other authorities concerned recommended either a tunnel or a clear span bridge. For the bridge alternative it was required that it have a clearance of 41 meters above Highest High Water Level and that the piers should not extend into water deeper than two meters below Lowest Low Water Level. To conform with the other parts of the Expressway both bridge and tunnel alternatives needed to provide three traffic lanes in each direction. Also the gradient of the approaches and the bridge or tunnel should not exceed 5%.

In January 1980 the ETA contracted a consultants' joint venture comprising Peter Fraenkel & Partners, Parsons Brinckerhoff International Inc., Dr. Ing. Hellmut Homberg & Partner and National Engineering Consultants Co., Ltd. to prepare a comparative study and final design for a bridge or tunnel crossing of the Chao Phraya River at Wat Sai. This study was completed in October 1980.

RESULTS OF THE BRIDGE TUNNEL STUDY

Cost analysis was based on a study of construction costs, land acquisition costs and operating and maintenance costs. The conclusion was that a tunnel would cost 50% more than a bridge. The study also took into consideration environmental impact, Expressway alignment and interchange layouts, revenue and user costs and operating considerations such as susceptibility to closure. In most of these respects there were clear advantages for a bridge. Another major factor was that the study determined that bridge construction time could be expected to be one year less than a tunnel.

Hydrographic and topographic surveys undertaken during the study showed that a minimum distance between pier foundations of 410 meters would be required, and therefore a main span of about 450 meters was specified.

Detailed consideration was given to two alternatives: either a suspension bridge or a cable-stayed bridge. In each case the design was for a box girder steel bridge deck with an orthotropic deck plate construction. A box girder is a hollow rectangle that supports the roadway. An orthotropic deck is a stiffened steel plate used in long span bridges because it is lighter than the concrete slab which is more commonly used in short span bridges.

For both alternatives the approaches were to consist of a series of simply supported 50 meter spans using twin double T-section prestressed concrete decks.

A suspension bridge design was discounted for reasons already mentioned. The final recommendation was for the 450 meter main span cable-stayed bridge with single plane configuration of cables anchored in steel pylons on each side of the river. Side spans, or anchor spans, of 61.2, 57.6, and 46.8 meters are provided on each side between the main span and the concrete approaches. The pylons are supported on large hollow concrete piers. The side span piers are of solid concrete to provide additional weight for anchorage (in this way the side spans together with their piers form a counter weight for the main span with the pylons acting as a fulcrum). All the piers are supported on 2 meter diameter bored piles.

DETAILED DESIGN

The design, which was undertaken between 1980 and 1981, drew heavily on Dr. Homberg's previous well known cable-stayed bridges, and in particular on the Friedrich Ebert Bridge in Bonn of which it is in many respects a magnified version.

As the pylon piers of the main bridge are situated on the banks, their effect on the river in terms of flow, erosion and mud deposits is minimal. The possibility of local erosion in the vicinity of the piers is prevented by rip-rap bank protection. Ship impact would not cause damage to the bridge because of the location of the piers and the massive pile caps that support them.

In addition to its own weight, which is about 10,000 tonnes, the main span of the bridge is designed to carry traffic (or "live") loading to the German Standard DIN 1072, bridge class 60. This standard gives a higher loading than would be obtained from any comparable national standard and it is unlikely to be exceeded in any actual traffic situation. Even at this design loading, the cables are strained to only

MAEDA CONSTRUCTION CO.,LTD.

45% of their tested breaking load.

The structure has also been checked for earthquake loads resulting from a horizontal acceleration of 0.05g, and wind loads appropriate for the location.

As it is a well known fact that heavy structures tend to sink in the Bangkok area, the design allowed for relative settlement of the pylon piers of up to 20 cms and up to 2.5 cms of the anchor span piers. Greater settlement

spirally during manufacture (locked coil cables) or they are simply laid straight side by side in a plastic tube (parallel wire cables). At the time the detailed design was being undertaken, the manufacture of suitably large diameter locked coil cables became feasible at lower cost than parallel wire cables. As locked coil cables have a better track record in terms of resistance to fatigue and corrosion, they were adopted for the final design.

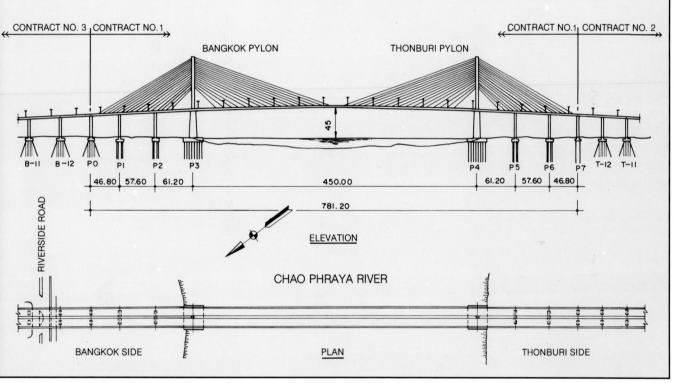

General Arrangement

can be accommodated by adjustment of the special rocker supports which connect the piers to the bridge deck.

The shape of the bridge deck was chosen from experience to give the best stability against vibrations caused by wind (aerodynamic stability). Wind tunnel tests were also called for under the construction contract to confirm the design's stability and to determine whether any additional measures would be necessary in this respect. Space was provided both in the pylons and in the bridge deck for the installation of 'dampers' should these be required. These dampers consist of a hanging mass arranged to reduce wind induced vibrations.

There are currently two methods of making prefabricated large bridge cables. The individual high strength cold drawn steel wires are either coiled

The detailed design and preparation of tender documents was completed towards the end of 1982. Contracts for the Port - Dao Khanong section of the Expressway were divided into two parts comprising four contacts each. The division of Part 1 was as follows:

Contract 1   The Cable-stayed Bridge
Contract 2   Thon Buri Approach
Contract 3   Bangkok Approach
Contract 4   Suksawat Interchange

Following further negotiations, the Consultants' Joint Venture was awarded another contract to be the supervision engineer for the construction phase.

DESCRIPTION OF THE BRIDGE

BRIDGE DECK AND PYLONS

The main section of the bridge deck is a three-cell steel box girder 21.8 meters wide and 4 meters deep at the center. The central cell houses the cable anchorages of the bridge deck. The side cells are supported by the central cell. Deck panels projecting from the box girder complete the cross section.

The 87 meter high pylons pass through the bridge deck without structural connection. The pylons have flared bases which are held down on the 6 meter thick caps at the heads of the pylon piers by long tensioned high strength bars. The four high yield steel plates which constitute the base section are 100 mm thick. The thickness of the

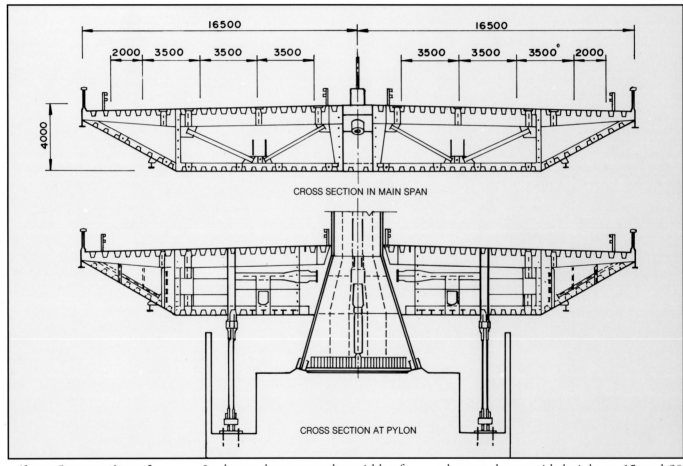

CROSS SECTION IN MAIN SPAN

CROSS SECTION AT PYLON

Above: Cross sections of bridge deck in main span and at pylon

Top Right: Anchor span cross sections

In the anchor spans the width of the bridge deck increases from 31 meters to 33 meters in order to pass the pylons with sufficient clearance. The cantilevered deck panels increase in width from 4.6 meters at the junction with the approaches to 5.6 meters at the pylons. In the main span a sloping web extends from the base of the box girder to the outer edge of the 5.6 meter deck panels to form the aerodynamically streamlined shape.

The longitudinal stiffening of the bridge deck is generally by U-shaped ribs welded to the insides of the plates. Transverse stiffening is by built-up T-shaped beams spaced at 3.6 meter intervals which, with the diagonal tubes, are also part of the deep transverse load spreading frame.

plates reduces with height to 15 and 20 mm at the pylon top.

The bridge deck is supported on the piers by "pendels" (also known as "rockers"). These are heavy fabricated members, with 400 mm diameter pinned connections at each end, which allow the bridge deck to expand and contract freely. In the completed condition the pendels at the junction and anchor span piers are in tension (holding the deck down) while those on either side of the pylons (at the pylon piers) are in compression (supporting the deck). The main purpose of the pendel supports to the bridge deck at the pylon piers is to resist any twisting forces from uneven traffic loading on the main span.

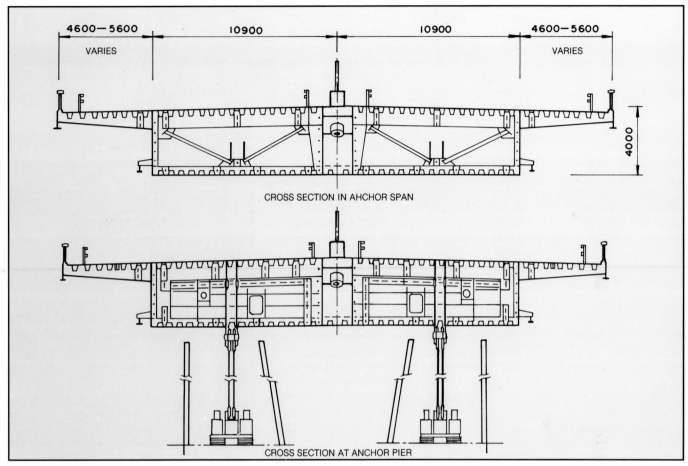

4600—5600 VARIES

10900

10900

4600—5600 VARIES

4000

CROSS SECTION IN AHCHOR SPAN

CROSS SECTION AT ANCHOR PIER

THE SUBSTRUCTURE

Bangkok is situated in the southern end of the Chao Phraya flood plain and rests upon several hundred meters of alternate strata of clay, sand and gravel above the bedrock. Sixteen meters of soft compressible clay form the surface which is undergoing subsidence due to deep well pumping.

The bridge site is 13 kilometers from the sea. The ground consists of a weathered clay crust some 1.8 meters thick, overlying 13 - 14 meters of soft recent marine clay which is followed by 8 - 10 meters thickness of Pleistocene stiff clay. This rests on a sand layer 24 - 37 meters deep on the Bangkok side and 25 - 44 meters on the Thon Buri side.

The pylon piers of the bridge are supported by 64 bored piles with a diameter of 2 meters. The tips of these piles are embedded in the first sand layer at about 30 meters below mean sea level on the Bangkok side and 35 meters on the Thon Buri side. The anchor span piers and one junction pier are founded on eight or ten of the same

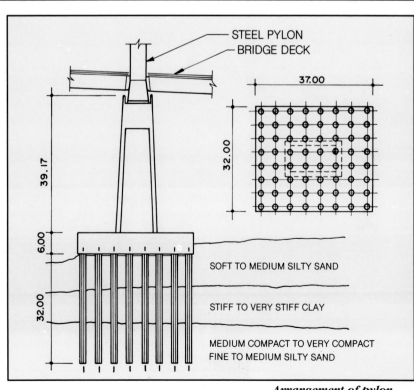

STEEL PYLON
BRIDGE DECK

37.00

32.00

39.17

6.00

32.00

SOFT TO MEDIUM SILTY SAND

STIFF TO VERY STIFF CLAY

MEDIUM COMPACT TO VERY COMPACT
FINE TO MEDIUM SILTY SAND

Arrangement of pylon pier and foundation

type of bored piles. The Bangkok side junction pier foundation was changed to driven piles to reduce delay during construction.

The piles for the pylon piers are surmounted by massive solid concrete pile caps. These are 6 meters thick, 37 meters wide and 32 meters long and contain approximately 18,000 tonnes of concrete.

The pylon piers are hollow reinforced concrete structures. The walls are 1 meter thick and 29.7 meters high. Load bearing caps 6 meters thick support the pylon. The anchor span piers are of solid reinforced concrete, designed to act mainly as counterweights, holding down the deck. This is because the main span is longer than the total length of anchor spans on both sides of the river. Hollow junction piers are provided at the junction between the steel bridge and the concrete approach viaducts. At the top of these piers a special sliding "wind shoe" bearing is provided to resist lateral (wind and earthquake) forces from the bridge deck ends. 1,200 tonne capacity sliding bearings are also provided for this purpose at the pylon bases.

CABLES AND ANCHORAGES

The bridge deck is supported by four sets of 17 cables with diameters varying from 121 mm. (the shortest) to 167 mm. (the longest). The minimum breaking load of the 167 mm. cables is 2,800 tonnes. These are, in terms of cross sectional area and breaking load, about twice as big as any previously used.

Locked coil cables were chosen because of their technical superiority, economy, long life, and successful

Right: Cross section of largest locked coil cable (167 mm diameter)

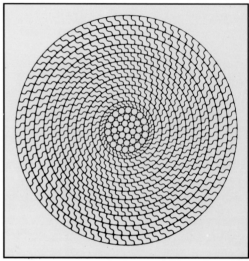

Below: Pylon and deck details

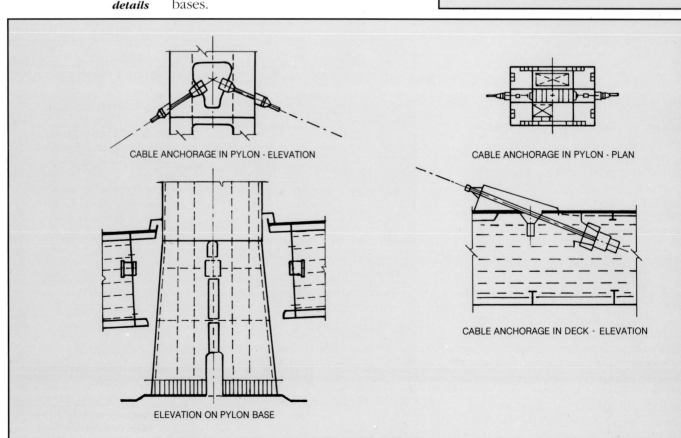

CABLE ANCHORAGE IN PYLON - ELEVATION

CABLE ANCHORAGE IN PYLON - PLAN

CABLE ANCHORAGE IN DECK - ELEVATION

ELEVATION ON PYLON BASE

world-wide track record on completed bridges. They were manufactured by Thyssen Draft AG of West Germany.

To achieve optimal corrosion protection the wires that make up the cables were individually galvanized. Voids between the wires were entirely filled by an active zinc-based paste during manufacture. A final protective treatment was applied by brush after the excess zinc paste was extruded, a process that takes place after the cables have been put in place and stressed.

Prestretching, marking and cutting of the individual cables was carried out on a special bed. This was followed by coiling and socketing. The heaviest coiled cable had an outside diameter of about 7 meters and weighed about 40 tonnes. It was in this form that they were shipped from Germany.

Because of the unprecedented size of both cables and sockets, unusually strict quality control measures were exercised. The physical properties, such as modulus of elasticity and breaking load, were determined by testing a short test length taken from each production run.

The cables are anchored into the pylons by simple hammer head sockets. Anchorage cutouts are formed in two 50 mm thick internal plates extending over the upper 55 meters. In the bridge deck the cables are anchored by cylindrical sockets with supporting collars. The sockets, weighing up to 1.5 tonnes, were cast from special steel in Germany and fitted to the cables before shipment.

CORROSION PROTECTION

Except for the final coat, the protective treatment for the fabricated steelwork was applied entirely by airless spray at the fabrication factory. Fabricated panels were sand blasted and treated with one coat of zinc/epoxy primer. During the assembly process red lead/epoxy primer was applied in two coats on external surfaces and one coat on internal surfaces followed by a brush-applied red lead and micaceous iron oxide (MIO) epoxy stripe coat at plate and stiffener edges. External surfaces then received two coats of MIO/epoxy, and internal surfaces one coat, to complete the shop treatment.

After erection, the paint system was made good at joints and any damage repaired. A polyurethane based finishing coat was applied to external surfaces by airless spray. The final dry film thicknesses were 270 um and 210 um on the external and internal surfaces respectively.

SURFACING, WATERPROOFING AND DRAINAGE.

On both the steel bridge and the approaches the road surfacing is the same as on the other parts of the Expressway. It consists of regulating and wearing courses of asphaltic concrete with a combined thickness of 70 - 80 mm.

For the steel bridge a special waterproofing layer of tar-epoxy-urethane was applied. This was laid by Perfect Built of Bangkok with materials supplied by CIS Paris of France.

The roadway drainage gullies feed into galvanized steel drainpipes which run through the girder discharging at the pylon and junction piers.

All electrical cables for bridge services (internal lighting, floodlighting, signaling, CCTV etc.) are carried in steel trunks or conduits.

CRASH BARRIERS

A special barrier, with two hollow steel rails, was developed for median and outer crash barriers, utilizing sections cold formed in Bangkok by Sahayont Steel Pipe Co., Ltd. The barriers were fabricated and erected by TESCO and ACME Construction Co., Ltd. both of Bangkok. Outside the outer barriers is a narrow walkway for maintenance and inspection personnel which is protected by a steel handrail. A wire rope is contained in the top member of this handrail to provide additional stopping power in the unlikely event of an errant vehicle penetrating the crash barrier.

MAINTENANCE ACCESS AND NAVIGATION LIGHTS

In addition to ladder access, the pylons are equipped with small service lifts giving access to seven levels, the highest being within seven meters of the top. There the stiffened pylon skin plates are carried one meter beyond the top diaphragm to form a safe working platform from which closed circuit television cameras, provided for monitoring expressway traffic, and the top set of aircraft warning lights can be serviced. There are two further sets of aircraft warning lights at intermediate levels. These are mounted on rotary

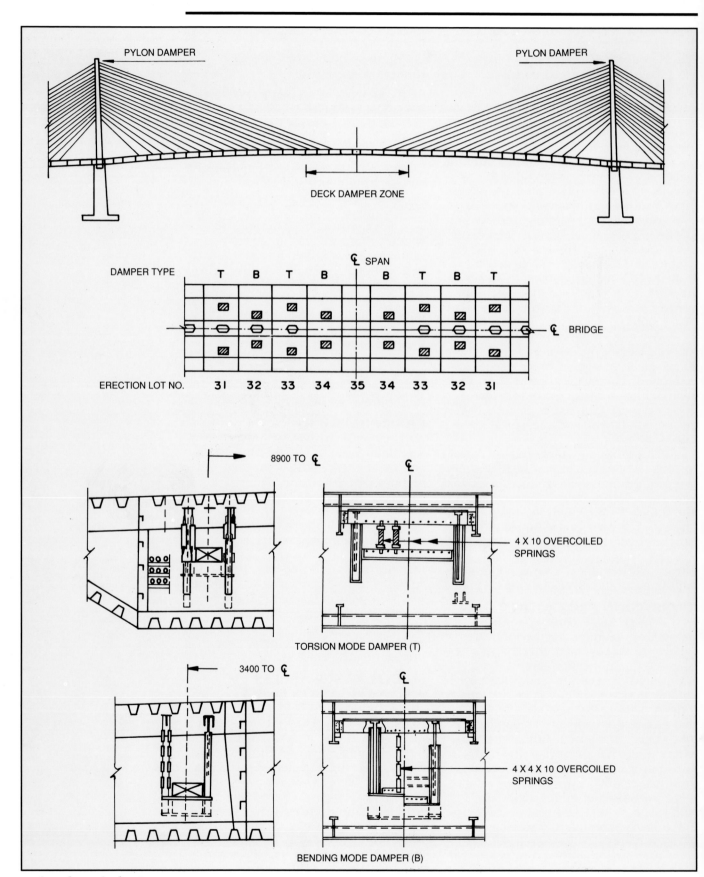

PYLON DAMPER

PYLON DAMPER

DECK DAMPER ZONE

DAMPER TYPE

	T	B	T	B		B	T	B	T	

℄ SPAN

℄ BRIDGE

ERECTION LOT NO.   31   32   33   34   35   34   33   32   31

8900 TO ℄

℄

4 X 10 OVERCOILED SPRINGS

TORSION MODE DAMPER (T)

3400 TO ℄

℄

4 X 4 X 10 OVERCOILED SPRINGS

BENDING MODE DAMPER (B)

Aerodynamic dampers

arms to permit servicing from inside the pylon. Lightning protection is by a 10 meter high flag mast mounted centrally on the top platform and equipped with a special decorative lightning tip housing a further aircraft warning light.

The deck box girder is equipped with two internal steel walkways for maintenance and inspection. Manholes are provided giving access between the girder cells at suitable intervals and also into the pylon base and onto the piers.

Four rails are provided for a powered maintenance inspection gantry. This consists of two half gantries so arranged that the piers can be passed by withdrawing telescoping sections.

AERODYNAMIC DAMPERS

The aerodynamic effects of wind on the bridge deck and pylons were studied in wind tunnel tests and records of wind speed and direction at 50 meters above Mean Sea Level were also made during the construction period.

The tests were conducted using models of the bridge deck and pylons at the Hitachi Zosen Corporation's Structural Research Institute at Osaka, Japan. Limited oscillations of the deck model were observed only with wind blowing with an upward component. These oscillations would not be dangerous for the bridge, but it was thought that, if they occurred, they might become noticeable or uncomfortable to users, and might possibly cause traffic accidents. To avoid any possibility of this happening it was decided to install tuned mass dampers in the bridge deck. Similar tests indicated a need for dampers to counter the possibility of lateral wind induced oscillation of the pylons.

The tuned mass dampers consist of a mass hanging from tension springs with "viscodampers" attached (the viscodampers comprise cylinders, attached to the mass, containing a viscous fluid in which a plunger, attached to the bridge, is immersed). They are tuned to the natural frequency of the bridge, and if wind induced oscillations begin they reduce the amount of movement of the bridge by themselves moving and so absorbing energy.

There is one damper in each of the pylons, immediately above the top cable anchorages. The deck contains

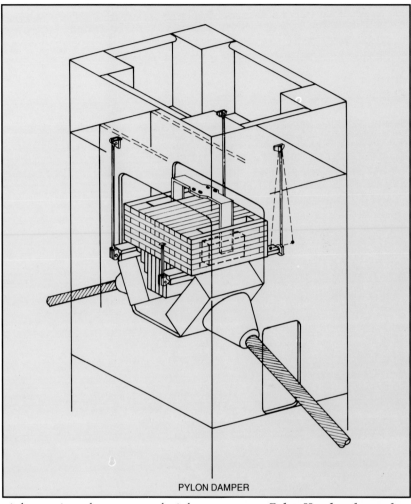

PYLON DAMPER

Pylon Head and aerodynamic damper arrangement

eight torsion dampers and eight bending dampers each with a weight of five tonnes. Both in terms of weight and number of units this is the most extensive use of tuned mass dampers in any bridge built to date.

CONCRETE APPROACH VIADUCTS

TENDERING FOR BRIDGE AND APPROACHES

Prequalification notices were issued for the four Contracts of Part 1 of the Dao Khanong Expressway in August 1981. Invitations to tender for the Cable-stayed Bridge, Thon Buri Approach Bridge and Bangkok Approach Bridge were issued to 18 pre-qualified contractors on 7th September 1983. Tenderers were permitted to submit alternative tenders in respect of modifications to the Specification or alternative designs and also completion in 3, 3.5, or 4 years. The closing date for the receipt of tenders was 21 December 1983.

Fourteen contractors and joint venture consortia submitted tenders for various combinations of the three contracts and for the Engineer's and alternative designs.

The Consultants recommended that a detailed assessment should be made of a limited number of viable tenders. This recommendation was accepted, and a detailed examination was carried out of the five tenders for Contract Nos.2 and 3 (three for the Engineer's design and two for alternative designs).

For Contracts 2 and 3 the lowest tender was for an alternative design which could not be recommended as it was the Engineer's opinion that the savings were the result of under-estimation of pier reinforcement and pile capacity.

The lowest tender for the Engineer's design was for a period of three years. There were a number of contractual qualifications to be clarified but subject to this the Engineer was able to recommend its acceptance. The successful tenderer was the "Consortium Chao Phraya" consisting of Ishikawajima-Harima Heavy Industries Co., Ltd. in joint venture with Maeda Construction Co., Ltd., Kawasaki Heavy Industries Ltd. and Mitsubishi Heavy Industries Ltd. Three of these Companies, who were steel fabricators hoping to win Contract No. 1, dropped out of further active involvement, so that Maeda Construction Co., Ltd., became effectively the Main Contractor. The finally accepted tender was for Baht 493,708,392.

The same consortium was later awarded Contract No.4 for the Suksawat interchange with a contract period of 30 months. All contracts were scheduled for completion by 30th September 1987.

DESCRIPTION OF THE APPROACHES

The concrete approaches are dual double-T post-tensioned simply supported concrete girders. There are

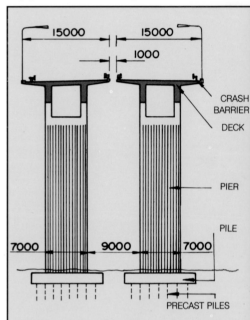

13 spans on each side of the river, all 50 meters long except for two spans connecting to the bridge on the Thon Buri side which are 40 meters long. Each approach road is 15 meters wide with three lanes contained by median and outer crash barriers.

Except at their lower ends, where vertical curves provide the transition to flat at-grade sections of the Expressway, the bridge approaches are on a 5% grade, rising from an elevation of 3 meters to a height of 39 meters at their junction with the cable-stayed bridge.

Reinforced concrete box-section piers were found to offer the least costly solution. To accommodate the imposed loads and provide adequate seating for the double T-section deck each pier needs to be 6.5 meters wide by 3 meters deep and to have a wall thickness of some 0.3 meter.

Approach Viaduct cross section

The piers are provided with access doors and internal steel ladders leading to the pier caps to facilitate inspection and maintenance of the deck bearings. The bearings themselves are designed for ease of replacement with stainless steel jacking plates cast into the deck webs over the ends of the bearing plinths.

The reinforced concrete piers and pile caps are supported on driven concrete piles of 0.525 x 0.525 meter section and 20 -25 meters in length. Steel raking piles are 0.356 x 0.368 meter H-section and 27 - 30 meters in length. The piles are driven through the clay layers into the top of the first sand layer.

Raking steel H-section piles were used to carry earthquake and other horizontal loads.

DECK CONSTRUCTION

The method of erection adopted was that envisaged by the designer and for which the double tee design had been specifically developed, mainly in Europe: in it, a special structure, capable of being "launched" forward from span to span, is used to support steel formwork. Arrangements are made within the system for the whole structure, complete with its formwork, to be jacked down onto rollers after a deck cast in it has been completed. In this way it can be launched forward into the next span ready to start again. This system becomes economically attractive in a case where there is a large number of identical spans to be cast in a repetitive operation.

Two "launching gantries" were used, one on each side of the river, giving 26 uses for each gantry in two runs of 13 each. The specialized design work was done in Japan by Tomoe Kikai Kogyo Co., Ltd. who also supervised fabrication, erection, and commissioning in Thailand. The 2,000 tonnes of complex steelwork for the two gantries were fabricated by Sino-Thai Engineering and Construction (STECON) in their existing factory in Bangkok. This was accomplished in a tight four month programme. The steel material was imported from Japan and all the elements were trial assembled before delivery; the site connections were by High Strength Bolts.

The gantries, some 108 meters long and weighing over 900 tonnes, consisted of three large steel box girders each with a truss "nose" and "tail" and each with two heavy steel rails on its underside. The girders were divided into short sections suitable for transport to the site and for later dismantling and re-erection. A set of high capacity tubular support towers was also provided to carry the outer two girders during launching and casting; the system was carefully devised to be able to cater for all the various pier heights. After casting and stressing a new span, the T-beam side shutters were withdrawn by hydraulic rams and the whole gantry lowered onto sets of rollers on the three piers and their associated falsework towers. The gantry was then moved up the slope by another set of hydraulic rams reacting on high strength steel rods attached to the front of the newly cast deck.

The complex gantries, complete with their hydraulic equipment and support towers, represented about 20% of the value of the viaducts they were to construct. They were so successful that they soon were able to advance at the rate of one span every two weeks instead of the three weeks originally planned. The time gained more than compensated for an initial delay in providing the equipment and for the extra time used up in dismantling and re-erection at the end of each carriageway length. The Bangkok side started first and remained ahead so that it was always the learning side. The detailed design was so good, however, that acceleration up to the two week cycle took place very quickly.

At the last deck on each line, it was not possible to launch the gantry in the normal way because the steel bridge superstructure was already erected and obstructed the noses. A method had to be devised to allow the noses to be dismantled during the launching operation with the gantry still safely supported at the front. Because the noses, which had to be reused, had bolted connections at eight meter intervals, it was necessary to provide an extra temporary support about nine meters from the final (junction) pier.

In order to avoid the need to build new foundations and temporary steel towers to provide this short term support, a method designed by a British consulting engineer was adopted. The method utilized temporary steel tower equipment which had just become available from the bridge contract, suitably modified to form a special leaning tower, or "Pisa tower" as it

Above: The casting gantry in use

came to be known.

This tower performed the dual function of providing the temporary support nine meters out during the final launch and also the support tower for concreting the final deck. It was constructed in the vertical position on knuckle bearings on the existing junction pier pile cap. It was then tipped out until an articulated link frame attached to the junction pier held it securely in position with its standard launching roller units about nine meters out from the face of the pier. The gantry was then launched forward step by step onto the leaning tower, a section of each of the three noses being removed by cranes after each step.

After four such "launching-dismantling" steps, the end of the truncated gantry was attached to the top of the leaning tower, and a final launching operation used simultaneously to right the tower and bring the gantry into its final working position. The Pisa tower was used for this operation four times, twice on each side of the river.

Right: The "Pisa Tower" before the final launch and righting operation

The final deck was then cast using the normal procedure and the gantry prepared for lowering to the ground, either for reuse on the second carriageway or for removal from site. This operation was carried out by VSL of Switzerland, using special heavy lift jacking equipment.

The whole gantry was first suspended using the special jacks supported on steel cross beams on the newly cast deck with support cables passing outside or through holes in the deck. The steel support towers were dismantled by cranes working on the ground below and the Pisa tower was rushed across the river for its next use. The two side girders were then lowered and touched down on prepared supports simultaneously, in such a way as to preserve balanced

loading in the steel cross beams above. Special arrangements had then to be made during the lowering operation of the center girder to remove first the section supported on the pier. The first of these lowering operations took 45 days, reducing to 35 for each subsequent occasion.

The final deck on Bangkok side was cast three months ahead of programme, and at Thon Buri one and a half months ahead.

Fitting of roadway expansion joints, erection of parapet handrails, crash barriers and street lighting, and surfacing operations followed within the remaining available time.

COMPARISON OF BRIDGE TENDERS

Tenders with a wide spread of values and variants were received from ten prequalified contracting groups. Following the Consultants' recommendation a detailed assessment was carried out of four tenders for Contract No.1 (three for the Engineer's design and one for an alternative design).

For Contract No.1 the lowest two tenders were both for alternative designs. These were rejected for a number of technical reasons.

The lowest tender for the Engineer's design was considered to be a viable tender which could be recommended for acceptance subject to clarification of a number of commercial and technical qualifications. This tender was for a period of 3.5 years. Meetings were held with this tenderer, the ETA and representatives of the Consultants during April 1984 as a result of which an acceptable tender emerged for a contract period of three years in the sum of Baht 924,579,000. The successful tenderer was a consortium led by Hitachi Zosen Corporation in joint venture with Chor Karnchang Co., Ltd., Kobe Steel Ltd. and Nissho Iwai Corporation - later known as the Dao Khanong Bridge Consortium, (DKBC).

Hitachi Zosen Corporation's successful tender for the Cable-stayed Bridge Project's superstructure was based on the use of as much local manufacture as possible. This option was dismissed as impracticable by all but one of the other seven tenderers in view of the lack of suitable existing fabrication facilities or experience in Thailand and of the short 42 month construction period originally envisaged. They would have fabricated at home and shipped completed steelwork for erection in Thailand. When the contract period was fixed at 36 months at the end of the tender negotiations, the task in hand seemed to many observers to be almost impossible to achieve.

Hitachi Zosen already had considerable experience of fabricating using local subcontractors on large steel structure projects in Asia, and considered that this would be the only way to achieve a sufficiently competitive tender price. There were three main areas of saving to be gained by using this approach. Adequate labour resources of sufficient skill were available at significantly lower cost than in Japan, or other industrialized countries. There were considerable import duty advantages to be gained by importing plate material as opposed to fabricated steelwork. The transport costs were also lower because of the much better volume ratio of plate compared with fabricated bridge elements. The combination of these factors meant that any tenderer willing to take the risk of fabricating locally would almost certainly beat any competitor fabricating abroad.

CONSTRUCTION OF THE BRIDGE

TIME SCHEDULE

With a contract time of only three years it was essential that construction work begin as soon as possible. This required the rapid commencement of foundation work and the establishment of a steel fabrication plant.

For Contracts 1, 2 and 3 (Steel Bridge and Approaches) the "Notice to Proceed" was issued on the 26th September with a commencement date of 1st October 1984 and completion in

The pylon pier cofferdams enclosed an area 34 by 39 meters. They consisted of a double wall of steel sheet piles with backfilling between them. Work on these began in January 1985 and the sheet pile walling was completed in March of the same year. The internal sheet piles had a length of 19 meters and the external ones a length of 15.5 meters.

At the end of March large deformations occurred in the outer

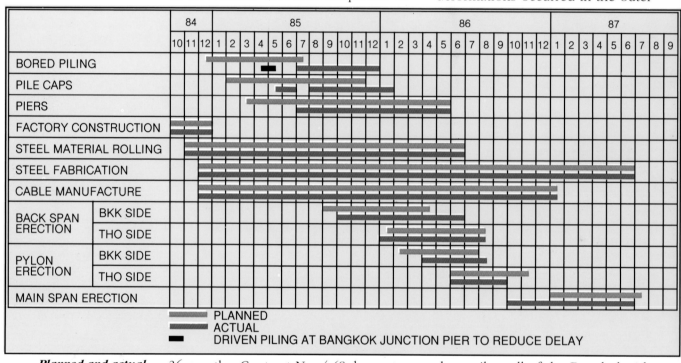

Planned and actual construction progress

36 months. Contract No. 4 (Suksawat interchange) started 6 months later with completion in 30 months.

Realizing the need for speed the contractors had begun work on site clearance in September which was before the official commencement date. For the steel fabrication plant work had started earlier, backfilling for the plant beginning in August and piling and steel frame fabrication already under way in September.

SUBSTRUCTURE

Before piling could begin it was necessary to construct cofferdams. These temporary structures consisted of steel sheet piles driven into the ground to provide a dry area for the permanent foundation work. Cofferdam work for the anchor span piers and junction piers was comparatively simple because they were situated on dry land. For the pylon piers the cofferdams had to be built in the river bank.

sheet pile wall of the Bangkok side pylon pier cofferdam. This was because clay in the river bed was softer than expected. To overcome this problem alternate sheet piles on the river sides were lengthened by seven meters. Also the level of the river bed was raised by placing boulders outside the cofferdam. This did not entirely solve the cofferdam problems and H - beam braces were also installed. Excavation was conducted on a block basis and oblique struts from the levelling concrete had to be installed as excavation proceeded to maintain stability.

All piers were founded on two meter diameter bored piles cast in situ under bentonite, and lined with steel over the top 15 meters. At the outset the contractor opted to use the reverse circulation drilling method, but one meter diameter instrumented test piles (which were called for under the contract to verify the design) failed. The cause of this failure was determined to be unexpected disturbance of the sand at the tip of the piles, caused by the drill.

Two measures were adopted to overcome the problem. The drilling method was changed to the auger-and-bucket method, a system which was in

use and available in Bangkok. Pile tip pressure grouting was also used as a means of restoring and consolidating the sand in the tip zone. The grouting was carried out after the completion of each pile by connecting high pressure grout pumps to a set of specially developed U-tubes which were cast into each pile during its construction. The effectiveness of the method was checked during the grouting operation by observing the completed pile rising under the influence of the pressurized grout at its base. Later one pile was also tested to 2,000 tonnes. Settlements of the completed foundations have been small. The pile construction and subsequent pressure grouting was carried out by Kin Sun Onward Co., Ltd. of Bangkok (a division of Franki, Hong Kong). In the course of solving the problem numerous pile tests were carried out by STS Engineering Consultants and Interconsult Co., Ltd. both of Bangkok.

Solving the piling problem was time consuming and permanent bored

piling started six months behind the original programme. This severe delay was overcome, however, by seven days a week, 24 hours a day, shift working on pile, foundation and pier construction. The early steelwork was erected onto the newly completed piers only a few weeks behind programme. In order to reduce the delay a little, the Bangkok side junction pier foundation was redesigned on driven piles which were supplied and driven by MCon Co., Ltd. of Bangkok.

After the cofferdams were excavated, the piles pressure grouted, and piles cut down to level, the reinforced pile caps were cast in single operations so as to avoid any danger of weak planes at construction joints.

For each pylon pier pile cap, the 7,100 cubic meters of concrete was cast

in a 40 hour operation. Since the pile cap is subject to constant wetting and drying within the tidal range as well as spraying by water of variable salinity, the specifications stipulated a maximum water-cement ratio of 45% and a minimum cement content of 320 kilograms per cubic meter to assure suitable durability.

To avoid the formation of a "cold" joint, the concrete in place had to be compacted together with fresh concrete well before the initial set. A retarding agent was added to prolong the initial setting time from three hours to six hours without affecting the strength of the concrete.

Five concrete mixing plants, each with a production capacity of 60-65 cubic meters per hour, supplied

Left: Construction of 2 meter diameter bored piles showing drilling rig and steel casing

Above: Preparation of pylon pier piles for pile cap construction

concrete for the pile caps. The required casting rate was 170 - 200 cubic meters per hour. There were two plants on full stand-by at all times. Two plants on the Bangkok side were only 100-200 meters from the location of the pour with the other three 2 - 9 kilometers away. On Thon Buri side the plants were at a distance of 1 - 10 kilometers. The travelling time through the erratic traffic was anywhere between five and 40 minutes.

In spite of the difficulties the sequence and rate of pouring was maintained with great precision, and

Concreting the Bangkok pylon pier pile caps

the concrete in place received fresh concrete well before the initial set. Fresh concrete was always placed against in situ concrete in less than one hour.

Different methods were used on various caps to prevent cracking caused by excessive temperature gradients within the pour. For the smaller back span pile caps closed off air gaps were kept around the sides of the pour and on completion the top was ponded and the whole tented over to reduce cooling air currents. The unit was continuously monitored electronically with thermocouples linked to a computer. All readings were recorded on disc for later analysis which confirmed that no critical temperature gradients had been reached. In the pylon pier pile caps water was pumped from the river and circulated through the pour in small steel pipes. This method proved very successful.

Because of the delay in

constructing the piles, the piers had to be constructed to an accelerated schedule as soon as the pile caps were completed. The pier formwork system chosen to meet this requirement was manufactured by DOKA in Austria and imported specially for the project. DOKA's local representative designed the detailed arrangement needed for each different pier shape, and the system adapted well even in complex situations. The main feature of the system allows rapid resetting of pier formwork from one lift to the next so that the lifting crane is most efficiently utilized. All setting and adjustment of the forms at a new level is carried out, using specially designed screws and clamps, from safe platforms incorporated in the units. The reusable plywood forms stiffened by special timber beams gave a high quality surface finish.

STEEL FABRICATION

The new factory at Samut Prakarn was built and operating in the first three months of the contract. The total output of 15,500 tonnes of permanent and 1,500 tonnes of temporary steelwork was completed in 26 months with a peak output of 1,150 tonnes in September 1986. With the exception of the diagonal bracing tubes and small section angle all steel was delivered from Japan as flat plate and fabricated at Samut Prakarn. All steel material was rolled for the project by Kobe Steel Co. of Japan.

Siam Machinery and Equipment (SME), one of the Ital-Thai Group of Companies, was subcontracted by Hitachi Zosen to undertake the fabrication work. SME had been involved with the only other tenderer who had intended to fabricate locally at the bidding stage. During the tender negotiation phase, Hitachi Zosen approached SME to bid as subcontractor for both fabrication and erection. SME already had considerable heavy building structural steelwork experience, and indicated their willingness to invest in a new, purpose designed fabrication plant. During these discussions and negotiations SME's senior managers visited Hitachi Zosen in Japan three times; at each successive visit, more and more detail was discussed and decided. The subcontract was finally signed on 22nd October

1984; backfilling for the new plant had started in August and piling and steel frame fabrication in September.

The design of the factory was based on an existing Hitachi Zosen plant in Japan. (at Mukaishima on Innoshima island in Hiroshima prefecture). Design, piling, and steel frame fabrication at SME's existing Bang Pa-in factory, North of Bangkok, proceeded concurrently. This plant had considerable heavy building steelwork experience and suitable steel sections were obtained immediately from the local market.

Arrangements were made for four of SME's key managers to receive practical training at Hitachi Zosen's factories in Japan. The training was tailored to the intended function of the managers concerned, and varied in length from 3 to 8 weeks.

Two of the group were accordingly specifically trained in the material ordering, shop drawing, material control, cutting plan, full size drawing, and steel tape and small part template production functions. The second pair were trained in all the production functions, spending 3 or 4 days on each of the steps from marking through to trial assembly and protective treatment application.

Extensive use was made of pictorial and video training materials, including only the essential descriptive English words. In this way the terms to be used for communication between the two groups on the shop floor were established. Similar materials were used for training subsequently at the shop. Later, a further engineer was sent for three weeks practical training in erection methods. He visited the erection planning department at Mukaishima works, followed by training at another plant where a large preassembly was effectively being "site" welded in the open, and finally the site of Yokogawa bridge where steel box girders were being erected using techniques similar to those planned for the anchor spans.

A team of 8 Hitachi Zosen supervisory engineers and one administrator, fully experienced in each production function, was to work full-time alongside the Subcontractor's local staff during the whole fabrication period. It is to their and their Thai counterparts' credit that, despite the need to communicate through the medium of English, fabrication to the necessary standards of accuracy and quality was carried out. Many long hours and weekends were worked to achieve this: all the supervisors were away from home on bachelor status.

On December 1st, 1984, the plant was commissioned, being sufficiently complete for fabrication to commence; The Hitachi Zosen supervisory team had taken up their duties a few weeks before. A programme of welder selection and testing for approval had been put in hand immediately, and detailed training using the pictorial aids was in hand.

Sufficient suitably experienced and capable welders were found and tested for various different classes of work: for the submerged arc and semi-automatic gas shielded equipment extensively employed throughout the plant special training was given. The welders' test failure rate was reasonably low, and there was no problem passing sufficient to meet the demands of the accelerating programme.

All the overhead cranes within the factory, and the two large gantries in the assembly area were fabricated and erected by SME to a programme designed to keep just ahead of the bridge fabrication and assembly requirements. Design and machinery supply for these cranes was by Toyo Kiden and Engineering Co. Ltd.

Plant and machinery for the factory were obtained either locally or from abroad and also commissioned to a rolling programme: the comprehensive list included a 6 meter shear and press for the U- rib section production, two large flame planers, a 3.7m x 6.7m capacity facing machine to be used for pylon unit and all other machining requirements, numerous drilling machines, and so on.

By January the total manpower level was already over 300, and it later peaked at over 600 during the time when both the bridge fabrication and work on steelwork for the first export contract was in the shop.

The first panels were completed by early February 1985, and fabrication output was already accelerating. Trial assembly of the first four blocks for Bangkok side was completed on 10th

July 1985, and the occasion marked by a ceremony attended by the Deputy Minister of the Interior and senior representatives of the organizations involved. This first test of the fabrication accuracy was passed successfully, and the methods used continued to prove themselves in all the remaining, varied fabrication work,

Lifting a main span block in the assembly yard

including the heavy machined pylon sections. The incidence of welding problems or defects was very low.

Outside the main factory a blasting shop and assembly area was established served by two 40 meter span 100 tonne lifting capacity gantry cranes. The assembly area incorporated piled support beams in its concreted working area so that the trial and final assemblies could be accurately supported. Completed blocks were removed from one end of each assembly while new ones were assembled at the other end. The assembly for each side of the river was arranged to move along the area in such a way as to minimize the need to move (and possibly reassemble) completed blocks.

After blasting and priming, protective treatment was carried out in whatever space was currently available outside or on top of the assembled steelwork using portable shelters designed for easy lifting by the gantry cranes.

Under the main Contract, Non Destructive Testing (NDT) had to be carried out by the Contractor: this was undertaken by the subcontractor's local staff with occasional training and cross checking by the Contractor's visiting expert or by Independent Inspection Companies as and when requested and agreed by the Resident Engineer. Radiographic and Ultrasonic techniques were used, together with Magnetic Particle and Dye Penetrant crack detection.

TRANSPORTING THE STEEL BLOCKS

SME was responsible for delivering all steelwork to the site, which for the anchor span and pylon elements presented no special difficulties: the steelwork was loaded into standard Chao Phraya river barges at the launching basins of Ital-Thai Marine, SME's neighboring sister company.

For the large main span blocks, weighing up to 200 tonnes, the original intention had been to extend the rails of the two 100 tonne gantries out into the river, so that the blocks could be loaded directly onto deck barges. This method had to be abandoned when it became clear that a small timber boat building yard's price for moving out of the path of the gantries would be too high.

The solution adopted to overcome this setback employed two purpose designed 5.5 meter gauge 100 tonne capacity bogies each equipped with a 2.5 meter diameter ball race turntable and made by SME. The blocks could then be moved transversely out of the assembly yard on a new set of rails, turned through 90 degrees, and loaded out onto the river transport along ITM's existing ship launching track. By using a single central jack at the crossover point of the new and existing tracks, the turning operation could be accomplished very rapidly, and on more than one occasion two blocks were moved out of the factory in this way in one day.

The early main span blocks were loaded in pairs into ITM's ship launching floating dock, in which they were then towed to the bridge site. During the latter part of the main span erection phase, however, ITM required their basin and floating dock for launching and preparation of the largest ship they had ever undertaken, which was also being constructed to a very tight programme.

The planned overall main span erection programme was achieved, and even slightly improved on, despite these new external constraints. It was fortunate that the erection cycle had been so well mastered by this time that block production had become the factor deciding the speed of construction: it was therefore possible to accommodate the transport "hiccups" caused by the ship launching and fitting out activities without any consequent overall delay.

OTHER LOCAL MANUFACTURE

High Strength Friction Grip bolts were specified for all site joints, except those in the deck plates, in diameters ranging from 16 to 36 millimeters. After extensive quality assurance checks, an established local company, Mahajak Industry Co., was accepted as the bolt manufacturer. All standard production quality control tests were carried out in Mahajak's testing labouratory and witnessed by the Resident Engineer's staff.

The contract called for Roller Shutter Roadway Expansion Joints at the junction of the approach viaducts and the steel bridge. These provide a level road surface as the steel bridge expands and contracts with temperature changes. On the Bangkok side the joints needed to be able to cater for movements up to plus or minus 40 centimeters.

It was required that the joints be produced by a recognized and experienced manufacturer and meet performance specifications. Manufacture requires large and accurate heavy machining capacity and considerable experience and it had therefore been assumed that complete units would have to be imported.

Hitachi Zosen had manufactured joints of this type in Japan after the expiry of the German patent and was one of the few companies in the world with the experience required by the contract. They decided, for these items also, to try to arrange for local manufacture. After some searching, a machine shop was located in Thon Buri which possessed two suitable planing machines and was experienced in their use. Neither machine was quite wide enough to accommodate the two meter wide and three meter long Bangkok side track frames. This problem was

overcome by the simple expedient of modifying one machine's tool portal so that a track frame, fixed to the standard moving bed, could just pass through. The modification was carried out with the close and detailed assistance of Hitachi Zosen's visiting machining expert, and was successful despite serious doubts experienced by the machine's original manufacturer.

The track frames with their special extra high strength machinable steel wearing plates were fabricated by SME at the new factory, together with the tongue and other roadway elements. All machining was carried out at the Thon Buri machine shop under the guidance of Hitachi Zosen's expert. The hardened steel pins and bushes connecting the moving plates were manufactured by Mahajak Industry Co. Anti-chatter springs were made by NHK Spring (Thailand) Co.

The joints were trial assembled at SME's factory where the fit-up gaps were checked and found to be within expected limits. Assembly, erection on site, and final fitting and adjustment of the moving parts was carried out by SME under Hitachi Zosen supervision.

ERECTION

Erection of the steel bridge followed the general method envisaged by the designer which was, firstly, to erect the anchor spans in small sections using temporary intermediate supports, secondly, to erect the pylons, and thirdly, to erect the main span as stayed cantilevers.

This method required a considerable amount of temporary steelwork for the temporary intermediate supports but it had time saving advantages over the alternative method of simultaneously cantilevering both sides out from the main piers. This was because construction of the substructure could begin with junction and anchor span piles, pile caps and piers. These could be constructed more easily and more quickly than the pylon piers. Another time saving factor was that the steel deck erection could start as soon as the first junction pier and intermediate support were complete.

The alternative of waiting until the pylon pier was complete, the steel pylon erected and the cables delivered would have meant a longer delay before starting deck erection. In order to speed erection the contractor decided to erect the main span steelwork in large 200 tonne completely prefabricated sections, 10.8 meters long. The 14.4 meter long anchor span sections, however, were assembled from smaller units on site after erection; this was the method originally envisaged for the whole bridge by the designer.

Thon Buri side erection was programmed initially to lag behind Bangkok side by four and a half months so that only one set of temporary steel bents would be required: as each section of the Bangkok anchor span was completed the temporary support bent would be dismantled and transferred across the river. In practice the lag was reduced to under three months for placing the first deck sections and progressively reduced to one month for the first main span lifts. As with the concrete approaches the lag also meant only one learning cycle for each new operation which was a very worthwhile principal to adopt. The local staff and labour force became rapidly proficient in the techniques and methods used, especially during the currency of the various repetitive processes. Learning time was also generally quite short as a result of the careful, detailed planning.

SME labour and site supervision was also used for erection, with another supervising team of Hitachi Zosen engineers producing detailed method statements and developing and finalizing scheme drawings from Japan. The major items of plant and equipment came from Japan together with three crane drivers for the main erection cranes. These cranes were newly manufactured for the project by Hitachi Construction Machinery Ltd. at their Tsuchuria works North of Tokyo. The first one was tested in Japan in June 1985 and ready for work on site in September. The other three and the pylon top cranes followed in succession as required.

Erection schemes and details were checked on site, with daily consultation and discussion. Head offices were of course always kept informed, and they were consulted, usually by telex or fax, in complex or high risk cases. Elevation control, with its associated complex computing, was carried out

and checked by the Head Offices concerned. In the case of the Consultant's checks and approvals, the 7 hour time difference between London and Bangkok allowed very rapid response to queries or new data: the answer to a question raised by one party in the evening could be on his desk the following morning.

The good working relations and the use of fax communication became particularly vital three weeks before the planned commencement of erection of the main span, when Freeman Fox Ltd. took over responsibility for checking and clearing the safety of the chosen big block main span erection method which Dr. Homberg, the designer, had been calling into question. The checking and information methods proved themselves in this situation, and main span erection commenced on schedule. Subsequent blocks were each also cleared only hours before erection, until the repetitive nature of the majority of the main span erection allowed the checking to achieve a more comfortable margin.

ERECTION OF THE ANCHOR SPANS

The first two sections of the anchor spans were erected piece by piece onto the junction pier and two temporary trestle towers by a KH-1000 crane: the central spine box unit was always erected first with part of the trestle tower missing to allow sufficient jib clearance at the required radius. For the second block, this first lift required the use of the special extra counterweight.

After completion of these first two blocks, the shifting rails, working deck and a complete KH-1000 crane were erected and assembled on top of the second: at Bangkok side Number 1 crane erected Number 2, while at Thon Buri a 300 tonne capacity Liebherr LT-1300 telescopic crane with lattice fly jib was available to lift Number 1 after its elements had been transported across the river by barge. The heaviest element in each case was the main machinery unit weighing 38 tonnes.

Subsequent erection was carried out by the deck mounted crane in cantilever, alternate sections being supported either on a permanent pier or on a temporary trestle tower. The central spine box section was always erected first followed by the two outer web units complete with lower runway beam; special "tension jig" devices were fixed on the deck plates before erection so that large high strength threaded rods could be used to carry the top flange tension force: in this way it was usually possible to release the crane from these elements after a few hours. Bottom compression and web shear were carried by the appropriate number of permanent bolts, inserted and tightened after location using drifts.

The remaining elements were then erected in sequence working from the bottom up until the complete cross section was in position, supported from the web elements by drifts and service bolts. The underslung gantry was then moved forward and all the longitudinal splices between the elements of the cross section were made. The

transverse splice between the finished section and its predecessor was then completed and the working deck and crane moved forward.

This was accomplished using purpose designed 320 tonne capacity jack sets working on shoes fixed by pins in a series of holes in the top flange of the box section shifting rails. The working deck cross beams were

supported with teflon lined bearing shoes on the stainless steel running strips on the top of the shifting rails. The movement speed was slow and well controlled, but it was possible to move forward within half a day.

The bottom and deck panels of the freely cantilevered sections and of those erected onto the temporary trestles were preassembled into approximately 8 meter wide units at

Above: Cantilever erection of anchor span lot 5

ground level before erection. The bottom panels of the sections straddling the piers were erected individually, and the Pendels were attached to their relevant panel before it was lifted.

For all these operations, the main cranes were assisted by a 90 tonne capacity Manitowoc W3900 crawler crane at ground level. This crane performed all unloading and material handling duties, and was moved back and forth across the river by barge as required. It was also used for erection of the third and fourth trestle towers. All steelwork, both temporary and permanent, was delivered to the site by barge, and small steel piled jetties were provided on each bank for unloading.

Erection proceeded on each bank in this way, phased in such a way that certain temporary works items could be re-used: such re-use was however limited by the exigencies of the tight programme. Six months were sufficient in each case to reach the pylon pier, where new procedures had to be used.

Left: Erection of lot 10 center block on to temporary tower

PYLON ERECTION

With the steelwork complete and the crane cantilevered from the last trestle tower to within centimeters of the newly completed pylon pier, pylon erection started. The base section, designated number 18, was delivered and erected in four quarters, each weighing 47 tonnes. A single unit

After completion of sufficient bolting of the flared base, two further one piece sections were erected, carefully aligned, and the joints welded.

At this point the crane reverted to deck erection, installing the complex lot 13 which surrounds the pylon base and included two particularly unwieldy heavy sections. These units

The erection scheme

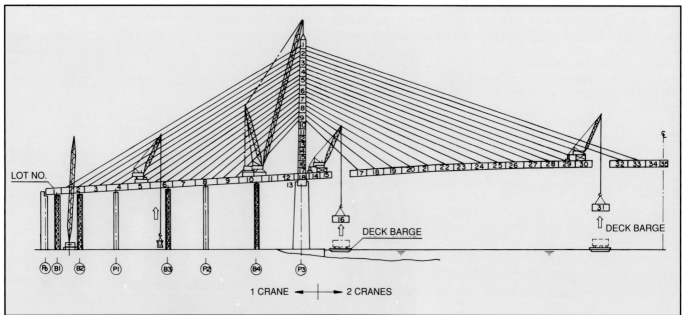

LOT NO.

DECK BARGE

DECK BARGE

1 CRANE ◄──┼──► 2 CRANES

Pylon erection - the first three blocks

would have been too heavy and too large. After unloading from their barges, these sections were upended by the deck mounted 200 tonne crane and the 100 tonne crane below working together. They were then lifted and positioned by the deck mounted crane.

incorporated the upper Pendel brackets, and the pins were partially inserted before lifting. The two pylon pier pendels had already been erected and their lower pins inserted before; they were left lying out of plumb in readiness. After completion of lot 13, the still cantilevered deck was raised by jacking at the head of the last trestle tower, the pendels pulled plumb into engagement with their upper brackets, the pins pushed home, and the tower released.

Erection of the two lots beyond the pylon was carried out by the piece by piece method concurrently with the start of pylon erection, the crane being suitably rigged with longer boom, but still standing at lot 11.

Erection of the remainder of the pylon was repetitive and straightforward, the crane being moved back, and its boom extended in steps. After the final section (lot 1) was in position the crane was used to erect the pylon top crane weighing 38 tonnes. This was clamped into position on the specially stiffened corners of lot 1.

The first pylon sections were unloaded by ground level cranes, but after the addition of its special counterweight the deck mounted crane was able to lift the sections directly from the river barge lying alongside the pile cap. A special extra long hoist rope had to be provided for lifting from the river with the 99 meter boom.

The sections were first lifted to the deck where they were dressed with the stagings required immediately for welding, and later for cable erection. While hanging, and before lifting into position, the lower machined plate edges were cleaned.

Positioning after lifting was facilitated by guides which had been welded at each corner during the trial assembly at the factory. These guides also served as the lugs from which the stagings hung, the tapered top parts being cut off after erection and setting. The machined joint accuracy was so good that the error at the top of the pylons after completion was no more than 20 mm.

After placing the sections in contact, half the thickness of the plates was joined by welding, and the internal stiffeners were connected by bolting.

Access to the top of the pylon during erection was by ladders connecting the external stagings. The permanent internal ladders were fitted later, after the internal welding and stiffener bolting was complete. Small service lifts were later installed in each pylon, under a separate contract, by Sun Thai Lift Co., Ltd. of Bangkok.

After completion of the superstructure, one of the KH-1000 cranes was rigged again twice with 99 meter boom, standing on part of the original enlarged working deck, and used to remove the pylon top cranes.

MAIN SPAN ERECTION

After completion of pylon erection, the KH-1000 crane was reconfigured with a standard 27 meter boom, and the remaining boom, mast and counterweight equipment was removed from the bridge deck. One half of the standard anchor span working deck, and all the additional working deck sections were also removed, leaving the crane on a half working deck on one side of the bridge. From this position, it was used to assemble the first of two new box girder working decks on lot 15. A new KH-1000 crane was then lifted onto the bridge from the ground, element by element, and assembled on the new working deck. In this case the crawler units were omitted and the crane's base unit was bolted directly to the working deck. This crane was equipped with a standard 27 meter boom and then used to assemble a second main span working deck on the other side of lot 15 and transfer its partner crane onto it, element by element.

The prefabricated deck lots and their associated cable stays were brought to site by barge from the fabrication factory 25 kilometers down river. Once the barge had been anchored in position the KH-1000 cranes mounted at the end of the deck cantilever lifted the cable stays onto the unreeling turntable mounted on the deck. The deck side units, which had been removed from the assembly before despatch from the factory in order to keep the main lift weight within the cranes' capacity, were also lifted onto the deck. The cranes were then locked in the straight-ahead position, and with their secondary counterweight lever systems connected,

Left: Erection of a pylon block

began the tandem lift of the preassembled lot.

During the lift the two crane drivers kept in continuous radio contact to ensure that they were sharing the weight equally. This was checked during the early stages by monitoring the cranes' automatic load cells, but once the lift was in progress, it was usually sufficient to synchronize the two cranes' winding rates.

The lot was brought into position and, after checks of line and level, bolted in place with sufficient service bolts to allow the cranes to be released. The side deck units were then lifted into place and the deck joints were welded. Finally, the remaining web and bottom flange plates and stiffener joints were bolted.

Meanwhile, erection of the backstay cable associated with the newly erected lot was in progress so that on the completion of the deck girder joints, erection of the complementary forestay could proceed.

Right: View from pylon showing unreeled and erected cables

Above: Deck end socket before cable erection

The cable coils were lifted to the bridge deck by the main erection cranes. They were placed in special unreeling devices supplied by the manufacturer and positioned just behind the cranes. Unreeling was carried out using a 10 tonne winch on the anchor span and special man-handleable support bogies. The main cranes loaded the coils into the unreeler, lifted the river end socket as it rotated to avoid damage to the emerging cable, and lifted the newly emerged part of the cable to allow the bogies to be inserted. After unreeling

and removal of protective wrapping the cables were inspected and prepared for erection.

Equipment was provided to ensure that the cables were never bent tighter than the recommended minimum radius of 30 times their diameter. A device known as the "Elephant's Trunk" was used to lift the upper end, the socket being released from the zinc cone and then loaded into Elephant's Trunk

which was lifted by the pylon top crane. During this operation, the cable was allowed to follow freely along the deck supported by its bogies. One of the main erection cranes was used first to raise and then to control the deck end of the main span cables. Anchor span cables were automatically controlled by the slope of the deck.

The Elephant's Trunk was attached to temporary lugs on the pylon face in such a way that the pylon end socket was offered up to the opening in the pylon. The socket was then drawn into the pylon by chain blocks. During this operation most of the weight of the cable was carried by the pylon top crane. One of the main erection cranes was used first to raise and then to control the deck end of the main span cables. Anchor span cables were automatically controlled by the slope of the deck.

At the deck end a curved support and sloping ramp was provided. The socket was first prepared by fitting the main 250 mm diameter screwed rod together with a string of up to three further 110 mm diameter rods joined by couplers. Winches were then arranged, suitably reeved up, and attached to a cable clamp close to the socket. Using this and the two erection cranes in the case of the main span cables, and a mobile hydraulic crane in the anchor span cables, the socket and string of screwed rods were carefully lifted and pulled until the cable could be laid over the curved support , and the string of rods fed into the deck and through the waiting stressing jack, with the socket lying on the ramp. During this, great care was taken to avoid overbending the cable at the socket. Winch forces of up to 120 tonnes were required for this operation.

Four 1,200 tonne jack units were provided by the Osaka Jack Co., Ltd. These were complete with pumps, remote control units, ram chairs,

manoeuvring trolley and sets of rails. They were purpose designed, tested and commissioned in Japan. Sets of screwed rods of the two diameters complete with couplers were provided. The screwed rod lengths were chosen to cater for the requirements of the final stressing of the largest cables as well as

for the clearance limitations of the smallest and most steeply inclined ones.

The jacks were first used to take the slack out of the cables, and the speed of operation was such that, once the screwed rod was inserted, a cable could be brought up to full stress in half a day. After reaching approximately the calculated load and extension in the day time the screwed rods were locked off. During the following night, bridge deck levels and cable forces were checked, the final decision on shim thickness taken, the chosen shims inserted, and the jacks released.

Above: 1,200 tonne cable stressing jack unit in use

The complete jack set was moved forward into the newly erected lot using small chain blocks, after the ram chair and jack set had been lowered onto their special bogie. After stressing, the Elephant's Trunk was carefully lowered from beneath the cable and the curved support and ramp moved forward for re-use on the subsequent cable.

The first two lifts of the main span (lots 16 and 17) were in some ways the most severe as the deck cantilever was, at this stage, unsupported by any cable stays. During the lift of lot 17 the free cantilever, supporting the two cranes and associated equipment weighing about 350 tonnes, was 30 meters long. After erection of the first pair of cable stays (one backstay and one forestay) the stresses in the deck became less critical and loading of the cables, particularly the leading pair, became the governing criterion.

Left: View from the pylon showing the "Elephant's Trunk" in use

SPAN CLOSURE

The two cantilevers steadily progressed outwards between September 1986 and May 1987 until just the final closing piece (lot 35) remained. At this stage it was necessary to move the Bangkok half bridge back longitudinally to provide clearance for the lot to be lifted into place. The temporary longitudinal bearings installed between the Bangkok pylon and the deck were replaced by hydraulic jacks with a total capacity of 600 tonnes. The jacks which had to act against both the elastic stiffness of the structure and the unbalanced longitudinal forces present in the deck at that stage, were used to pull the whole cantilever back 150 mm.

The two KH-1000 cranes on the Bangkok cantilever had by this time been dismantled, one for removal from site, the other for re-rigging and use at the pylon. The two remaining KH-1000 cranes on the Thon Buri cantilever carried out the final lift on 6th June 1987, as planned, during the early morning so as to minimize any reduction of the 150 mm setback clearance due to thermal expansion. With the final lot joined to the Thon Buri cantilever, the extra weight of the cranes and the final block caused a level difference at the final joint of 1.1 meters, exactly as predicted.

In order to remove this level difference, and make other preparations for the final joint, the remaining crane parts and other temporary and permanent works items were used as ballast to deflect the deck cantilever ends to the required profile. The ballast was also arranged to apply torques to the deck ends to correct the opposite twists of about 1 in 1000 which had developed in both cantilevers. Two jacking beams were provided to take out the final small level difference and to ensure a positive shear connection. The quantity of ballast required, 200 tonnes on the Bangkok cantilever and 160 tonnes on the Thon Buri cantilever, was considerably less than the weight of the KH-1000 cranes which had been present at the tip of each cantilever until the last lot on each side had been lifted.

After making various minor adjustments to the joint steelwork by machine flame cutting, the Bangkok cantilever was moved forward for the last time, offered up and joined to the Thon Buri cantilever during the night of June 15 by welding parts of the top and bottom flange plates and stiffeners sufficient to withstand the bending moments caused by temperature gradients in the deck which could occur on a sunny day. The temporary longitudinal restraint at the Bangkok pylon was released at this point, and welding of the remaining parts of the joint followed.

An all-welded joint was used in this case to facilitate adjustment and fairing of the joint and to obviate the

large amount of in-situ drilling which would have been required in a standard bolted joint.

The joint was completed during the main span closure ceremony attended by the Prime Minister of Thailand on 22nd June 1987, some 23 months after commencing superstructure erection.

Completion of the painting, crash barriers, and many other finishing operations took place in the remaining weeks.

Left: Lifting one of the final sections

Above: Lifting operation viewed from Thon Buri pylon

Top Left: 200 tonne erection cranes in action

Middle Left: Steelwork details revealed during the lifting operation

Left: closing the gap

APPENDIX

PARTICIPATING ORGANIZATIONS

CLIENT:
   The Expressway and Rapid Transit Authority of Thailand

ENGINEER (Design and supervision):
   A Joint Venture of: Design Responsibility :
   Peter Fraenkel International Ltd. (UK)   Contracts 2 and 3
   Parsons Brinckerhoff International Inc. (USA)   –
   Dr. Ing. Hellmut Homberg and Partner (W. Germany)   Contract 1
   National Engineering Consultants Co., Ltd. (Bangkok)   Contract 4 and landscaping

The Joint Venture appointed Freeman Fox Ltd. (UK) as Adviser and to take over the technical responsibilities of Dr. Homberg after his withdrawal shortly before commencement of main span erection.

MAIN CONTRACTORS:
   CONTRACT 1 – The Cables Stayed Bridge and its foundations
   The Dao Kanong Bridge Consortium, a Joint Venture of:
   Hitachi Zosen Corporation (Japan)   – superstructure
   Chor Karnchang – Tokyu Construction JV (Thailand)   – substructure, surfacing, landscaping, electrical
   Nissho Iwai Corporation (Japan)   – financial and business
   Kobe Steel (Japan)   – supply of steel plate

   CONTRACT 2, 3 AND 4 – The Approach Viaducts, ground level roads, and Suksawat Interchange
   Consortium Chao Phya, whose active member was:
   Maeda Construction Co., Ltd. (Japan)

SUBCONTRACTORS AND SUPPLIERS:
   CONTRACT 1
   Siam Machinery and Equipment Ltd. (Thailand)   – fabrication, erection
   Hitachi Construction Machinery Co., Ltd. (Japan)   – supply of main cranes
   Thyssen Draht AG (W. Germany)   – supply of cables
   Mahajak Industry Co., (Thailand)   – structural bolts
   Thai Kansai Paint Ltd.   – paint materials
   I.M.E. Co., Ltd.   – sand blasting and painting,
   Chugoku Co. (Japan)   – supply of urethane sealant
   GERB AG (W. Germany)   – aerodynamic dampers: design, springs
                                                                     and fluid

   Sahayont Steel Pipe Co., Ltd.   – crash barrier materials
   ACME Engineering Co., Ltd.   – crash barrier fabrication and erection
   Thonburi Loha Co., Ltd.   – machining expansion joints
   Kin Sun Onward Co., Ltd.   – bored piling and pile grouting
   Wattana Engineering Co., Ltd.   – pile grouting
   Thai Mui Co., Ltd.   – bored pile casing supply
   MCON Co., Ltd.   – driven piling at junction pier
   STS Engineering Consultants Co., Ltd.   – pile testing
   Interconsult Co., Ltd.   – pile testing
   SGS Far East Ltd.   – non-destructive testing
   Siwa Testing Inspection and Consulting Co., Ltd.   – non-destructive testing
   Intercon Contract and Consulting Services Co., Ltd.   – contractual advice
   DOKA (Austria)   – pier formwork
   Osaka Jack Co. (Japan)   – cable stressing equipment
   Saeng Pradit Co., Ltd.   – electrical cables and fittings
   Siam Cement Co., Ltd.   – cement supply
   CPAC Co., Ltd.   – ready mixed concrete supply
   Bangkok Steel Co., Ltd.   – reinforcement steel bar supply
   Philips Electrical (Holland)   – supply of flood – and festival lights
   Sun Thai Lifts   – pylon lifts
   Chu Chin Hua Co., Ltd.   – street lighting and pylon flagmasts
   Noppawong Construction Ltd. Part.   – asphalt paving
   Suwalee Co., Ltd.   – asphalt paving
   CIS Paris (France)   – supply of deck waterproofing material
   Perfect Built Co., Ltd.   – application of deck waterproofing
   Jack Tighe Autoblast (Singapore)   – blast cleaning of deck plate
   Advance Polymer Co., Ltd.   – neoprene cable coamings
   Secalt (Luxembourg) and Teo Hong Silom Co., Ltd.   – hoist and cradle for pylon and cable
   Kawaguchi Kinzoku Co., Ltd. (Japan)   – 1,200 tonne bearings at pylons
   C.B. Surveying Co., Ltd.   – contract survey services

Italthai Marine Ltd.	– launching basin and barge hire
Navarat Co., Ltd.	– barge hire
Bangkok Steel Co., Ltd.	– supply of steel reinforcement
Cleanosol Ltd.	– road marking
Sathupradit Sand Source Co.	– earthworks
Chongdee Construction Ltd. Partnership	– re-bar, formwork, concrete work
Marutai Co., Ltd. (Japan)	– cofferdam construction
Kito (Thai) Co., Ltd.	– mechanical parts for maintenance gantry
Mahasiri Co., Ltd.	– aggregate supply for concrete
Eastman Thailand Co., Ltd.	– crane lease
Thongsit Transport Co., Ltd.	– crane rental
Rompothong Engineering Co., Ltd.	– temporary steelwork fabrication and erection labour
Esso (Thailand) Ltd.	– supply of bitumen
Nam Saeng Engineering Co., Ltd.	– machine, equipment rental
Nava Service Ltd. Part.	– crane hire
Trailer Transport (1974) Co., Ltd.	– crane hire
Nisso Master Builders Co., Ltd.	– grouting materials for bridge bearings
Ua Withya Equipment Co., Ltd.	– galvanizing
Siam Steel Pipe Co., Ltd.	– galvanizing
Rompothong Engineering Co., Ltd.	– erection labour and tower fabrication
Siam Maritime Transportation (1987) Co., Ltd.	– floating crane hire
Inoue Rubber Co., Ltd.	– expansion joint sealing material
Winner Rubber Co., Ltd.	– expansion joint drainage trough
Tia Yong Saeng Ltd., Part.	– landscaping-pile driving
Hor Saeng Chai Co., Ltd.	– landscaping-pile supply
Udommongkol Construction Co., Ltd.	– construction of landscaping structures
Bangkok Foam Co., Ltd.	– polyurethane foam

CONTRACTS 2, 3 AND 4

Kay-Thai Engineering Co., Ltd.	– labour and formwork for piers
Sino-Thai Engineering & Construction Co., Ltd. (STECON)	– manufacture of deck casting gentries
Thai Tennox Co., Ltd.	– pile driving
Interconsult Co., Ltd.	– pile testing
The Metropolitan Concrete Products Co., Ltd. (MCON)	– precast prestressed concrete piles
The Pathumthani Concrete Co., Ltd. (PACO)	– precast prestressed concrete piles
General Engineering Ltd. (GEL)	– precast prestressed concrete piles
Siam Cement Co., Ltd.	– cement supply
CPAC Co., Ltd.	– ready mixed concrete
Rig-Thai Engineering Co., Ltd.	– viaduct handrails and fences
Thaveesin Engineering & Shipbuilding Co., Ltd. (TESCO)	– erection and moving of casting gantries and fabrication and erection of crash barriers
Chu Chin Hua Co., Ltd.	– street lighting and CCTV masts
Wongwaiwit Engineering Co., Ltd.	– supply of machined bearing "shims"
R. A. Freeman	– design of "Pisa Towers"
VSL Heavy Lift (Far East) Ltd.	– lowering casting gantries
VSL (Thailand)	– prestressing
Thai Special Wire Co., Ltd.	– prestressing strand
Kawasho Corp.	– reinforcement bar
Thai Meidensha Co., Ltd.	– electrical works subcontractor
Mong Huad Heng Ltd.	– sign board fabrication and supply
Noppawong Construction Ltd. Part.	– asphalt paving
Cleanosol Ltd.	– road marking
Charoenwit Ironwork Ltd. Part.	– cast iron products
Siam Syndicate Trading Co.	– cast iron products
Chusin Concrete Material Ltd. Partnership	– concrete drain pipes
E.L. Trading Ltd. Partnership	– sand and sub-base supply
Nippon Pillar Co., Ltd. (Japan)	– 600 ton bridge bearings
Nitta/Expandite Co. (Japan)	– "Transflex" deck expansion joints
Cable Covers Ltd. (UK)	– Contract 4 neoprene bearings pads
SGS (Far East) Ltd.	– material testing
TOA (Thai) Co., Ltd.	– paint materials
Vivat Steel Wire Rope Co.	– safety wire rope for handrails
Tomoe Kikai Kogyo Co. (Japan)	– design of casting gantries and supply of associated hydraulic equipment
Esso (Thailand) Ltd.	– supply of bitumen
VSL (Switzerland)	– supply of prestressing anchorages, jacks